DK READERS

Level 3

Level 4

A Note to Parents

DK READERS is a compelling program for beginning readers, designed in conjunction with leading literacy experts, including Dr. Linda Gambrell, Professor of Education at Clemson University. Dr. Gambrell has served as President of the National Reading Conference, the College Reading Association, and the International Reading Association.

Beautiful illustrations and superb full-color photographs combine with engaging, easy-to-read stories to offer a fresh approach to each subject in the series. Each DK READER is guaranteed to capture a child's interest while developing his or her reading skills, general knowledge, and love of reading.

The five levels of DK READERS are aimed at different reading abilities, enabling you to choose the books that are exactly right for your child:

Pre-level 1: Learning to read
Level 1: Beginning to read
Level 2: Beginning to read alone
Level 3: Reading alone
Level 4: Proficient readers

The "normal" age at which a child begins to read can be anywhere from three to eight years old. Adult participation through the lower levels is very helpful for providing encouragement, discussing storylines, and sounding out unfamiliar words.

No matter which level you select, you can be sure that you are helping your child learn to read, then read to learn!

DK

LONDON, NEW YORK, MUNICH,
MELBOURNE, AND DELHI

Editor Julia Roles
U.S. Editor John Searcy

Reading Consultant
Linda Gambrell, Ph.D.

Subject Consultant
Eileen Westwig, MSc.
American Museum of Natural History

Produced by
Shoreline Publishing Group LLC
Editorial Director James Buckley, Jr.
Designer Tom Carling, carlingdesign.com

First American Edition, 2008
Published in the United States by DK Publishing
375 Hudson Street, New York, New York 10014

DK books are available at special discounts when purchased in bulk
for sales promotions, premiums, fund-raising, or educational use.
For details, contact: DK Publishing Special Markets, 375 Hudson
Street, New York, New York 10014, or SpecialSales@dk.com

A catalog record for this book is available
from the Library of Congress.
ISBN: 978-0-7566-4085-9 (Paperback)
ISBN: 978-0-7566-4086-6 (Hardcover)

Printed and bound in China by L Rex Printing Co., Ltd.

08 09 10 11 12 10 9 8 7 6 5 4 3 2 1

The publisher would like to thank the following for their kind
permission to reproduce their photographs:
(Key: b=bottom; t=top)
Alaska Stock: 7, 12,13t; Animals Animals: 10; Corbis: 6, 37, 42, 43, 45,
46; Dreamstime.com (photographers listed): 13b, Steve Byland 16, Chris
Turner 23t, Spydr 25, Mike Rogal 39, Shady365 40; iStock: 4t, 5t, 18, 19,
22, 23b, 38; Gwich'in Social and Cultural Institute 10b; Minden Pictures
(photographers listed): Patricio Robles/Sierra Madre 4, Konrad Wothe 5,
26, Micho Hoshino 11, 14, 33b, Frans Lanting 20, 28, 35, Hiroya
Minakuchi 29, Sue Flood/npl 30, Flip Nicklin 33t, 34; Photos.com: 9.
Maps by Robert Prince.

All other images © Dorling Kindersley Limited
For more information see: www.dkimages.com

Discover more at
www.dk.com

Contents

READING
3
ALONE

Amazing Animal
Journeys

Written by Liam O'Donnell

DK Publishing

Animals on the move

Imagine walking from one end of your country and back again! You'd be pretty tired when you got home. Every year, animals around the world travel amazingly long distances. Their journeys are called migrations.

Some animals migrate to find food. Some travel to give birth away from predators. Other animals migrate to avoid cold winter weather.

Every type of migrating animal follows its own individual migration route year after year, whether by walking, swimming, or flying. Every migration journey is filled with risks, dangers, and adventure. This book tells the migration story of four different animals in North America. Turn the page to start the journey and join the amazing animal migrations.

Caribou

Springtime sunshine rises over a gently rolling river in the Yukon in northern Canada. Huffing snorts echo from the spruce trees that line the river. What animal lives in this chilly forest?

One by one, the animals step out from the trees. They have brown and gray fur, with short antlers that will grow much bigger later in the year. The animals are barren-ground caribou, one of three types of caribou found in North America.

Nearly 1.2 million barren-ground caribou live in eight large herds spread across northern Canada and Alaska.

These caribou are part of the Porcupine herd. There are 130,000 caribou in the Porcupine herd, named after the area around the Porcupine River.

Barren-ground caribou are about 4 feet (120 cm) tall at their shoulders and can weigh up to 300 pounds (140 kg). Their short, thick bodies help keep them warm in the cold Arctic weather. Their long legs and large hooves are perfect for the long distances they travel every year.

It is April. In a few weeks, it will be summer. The snow will melt from the tundra, far away in northern Alaska. Shrubs, flowers, and mushrooms will grow on the tundra. The caribou will walk for many weeks to reach these nutritious plants.

The bulging belly of a female caribou, called a cow, shows another reason for the migration. She is pregnant, but cannot give birth here. There are too many predators, such as wolves and bears. The pregnant cow must

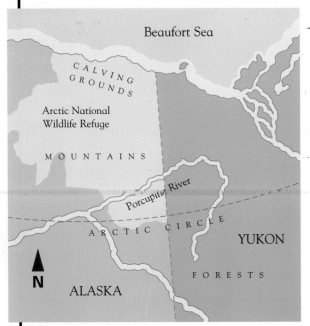

The Porcupine caribou herd migrates from the Yukon forests to the Beaufort Sea coast, and back again.

walk to the calving grounds hundreds of miles away. There, she and her newborn calf will be safe.

This cow is not alone. Other pregnant caribou in the herd are also eager to leave. If their calves are born before they reach the calving grounds, there is a higher chance the calves will not survive.

A few cows begin to walk north. It is time to leave. The spring migration of the barren-ground caribou is finally getting underway.

By early June, the caribou cows have spent six weeks walking through deep snow, crossing icy rivers, and climbing steep mountains. Along the way they have been hunted by wolves and grizzly bears. Finally, they arrive at the calving grounds on the coastal plain of the Beaufort Sea. The cows are safe here, in

Sharing the land

The Gwich'in people live in the migration path of the Porcupine caribou herd. Gwich'in means "people of the caribou." The caribou is part of their culture.

the Arctic National Wildlife Refuge in northern Alaska. Melting snow makes the ground too wet for wolves and grizzlies to move or make dens.

All across the wet ground, thousands of pregnant caribou cows lie on their sides giving birth. Our cow is one of them. When her calf is born, it is wet, small, and shiny. Immediately, the newborn calf struggles to its feet. Within minutes it is standing and suckling from its mother.

By the end of its first day, the calf is walking. Within a few weeks, it can run long distances. The calf is soon ready to finish the migration with its mother.

It is July. The calves are four weeks old and strong enough to follow their mothers on the rest of migration. The cows move off the coastal plain. They travel south to the foothills of the Alaskan mountains to meet up with the rest of the Porcupine herd.

The bull caribou started their spring migration a few weeks after the pregnant cows. Now, bulls, cows, and newborns are reunited.

Our newborn calf is hungry. It is eager to eat, but the summer heat brings millions of a different kind of predator: insects! Swarms of nose-

bot flies, mosquitoes, and warble flies torment the herd. The pesky insects aim for the skin of the caribou. They also try to bite the caribou's faces. To protect their vulnerable noses, caribou newborns huddle close to their mothers.

Pesky flies

Nose-bot flies plant larvae in the caribou's nostrils. The larvae crawl down the caribou's throat and can affect its breathing.

By early September, the swarms of bugs have decreased. The newborn caribou and its mother can now feed and begin their fall migration. The herd walks south and east, through the Alaska and Yukon mountains.

Tens of thousands of caribou spread across the late-summer tundra, feeding on grass, shrubs, and mushrooms. They must add fat to their bodies to help them through the cold winter months when food will be scarce.

During October, adult caribou begin to mate. This period is called the rut and it lasts only two weeks. During the rut, the caribou continue moving south.

By mid-November, the caribou arrive back at Porcupine River. Many months have passed since our pregnant cow started her spring migration. The forests of the Yukon will offer some protection during the long, cold winter. Next spring, the caribou will be ready to begin their migration north once again.

Monarch butterflies

One of the longest migrations could begin in your backyard. At the end of each summer, the Eastern monarch butterfly begins its migration from southern Canada and the northern United States. It flies all the way to southern Mexico, more than 1,800 miles (2,900 km) away.

The monarch is one of the easiest butterflies to recognize. Its thin, fragile, black body is smaller than a little child's finger. Its bright orange wings, with thick black borders covered in two rows of white dots, are easy to spot on a summer day.

Most monarchs live for only around 35 days. But at the end of summer, very special monarchs are born. These special butterflies live much longer and travel much farther than the monarchs born earlier in the summer. These special monarchs are migrating animals.

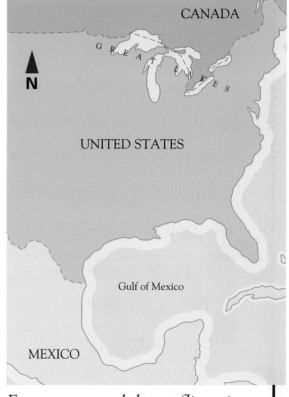

Eastern monarch butterflies migrate from around the Great Lakes to southern Mexico, and back again.

It is the end of August. A lone monarch butterfly flies across the blue Ontario sky. She does not flit back and forth, like the monarchs who lived before her earlier in the summer. This butterfly flies in a straight line. This behavior is called "directional flight" and it means that she is a migrating monarch.

She began her journey south at sunrise this morning and already she has traveled a long way. Monarchs migrate to escape the cold winter weather. They follow the same routes as

Monarch watch

You might find a monarch roost in your neighborhood! Look in the early evening, high in the trees around your home or in nearby parks.

many migrating birds, but
monarchs fly alone
and not in flocks
like birds.

Then, at
night, monarchs
gather together
in large
groups in
trees to rest
from their
long day of
flying. These resting groups are called
roosts. A roost can be small with only
a few hundred monarchs, or it can
be large with thousands of monarch
butterflies. Sometimes there are too
many butterflies to count in these
enormous roosts!

By the middle of October, our monarch has flown for almost seven weeks and traveled more than 1,800 miles (2,900 km). Along the way, she has roosted many times. She has also avoided many dangers, such as being blown off-course by fierce storms, or hit by moving cars. Finally, the monarch arrives in Mexico. She will spend the winter here and she won't be alone.

Every year at this time, the trees on twelve mountain peaks in central Mexico are covered in millions of orange-and-black monarch butterflies. They gather in the Mexican mountains and become almost dormant while they wait for the winter months to pass. The air is cool here, but not cold enough to hurt the monarchs.

It is February. The monarch comes out of her almost dormant state and joins the millions of other monarchs waking up. She spends a few more weeks in her winter home, and mates.

By the middle of March, the monarch flies north again until she reaches the Gulf Coast in the United States. There, she lays her eggs on a milkweed plant. Then she dies. For her, the long migration is over. But for a new generation, the journey is about to begin.

Monarch caterpillars are yellow, white, and black.

Caterpillars are born from the eggs. Later, a hard covering called a chrysalis forms around each caterpillar. When the chrysalis opens, a new monarch butterfly slowly emerges and

The monarch comes out from the chrysalis with its wings folded tightly to its new body.

spreads its wings. This monarch has never been to Canada, but something inside him tells him to fly north and continue the migration.

Milkweed

The monarch's favorite food is milkweed. There are more than 100 types of this flowering plant in North America. Yellow-flowering, swamp, and purple milkweed are found most often.

By May, the monarch arrives in Canada. He has flown more than 1,000 miles (1,600 km), feeding on milkweed plants. Summer is on its way, but this monarch butterfly will not be alive to see it. The monarch has just enough time to mate before he dies.

During the rest of the summer, two or three more generations of monarchs will be born. Each of these summer monarchs will live for only a few weeks, feeding on milkweed and flitting back and forth on the summer breezes.

Late in the summer, a special monarch will be born. Something inside her will tell her to fly straight. This young butterfly will fly a very long way to a place she's never been—just like her great-great-great-grandmother did only a year ago. The monarch migration will go on as it always has, and scientists will continue to study what makes this annual migration mystery keep happening.

Gray whales

Off the coast of Mexico, giants are on the move. Every spring, thousands of gray whales prepare to swim to Alaska, more than 6,000 miles (9,500 km) to the north, in search of food.

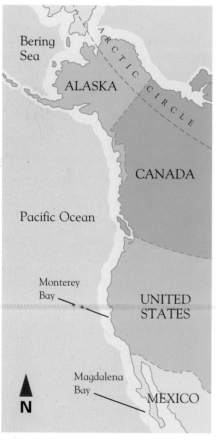

Gray whales are mammals. They feed on tiny marine animals that live in Alaskan waters. Gray whales can be 46 feet (14 m) long

Gray whales migrate from Mexico's Magdalena Bay to Alaska's Bering Sea, and back again.

and weigh 30–40 tons (27–36 metric tons). They get their name from the gray patches covering their thick skin.

The gray whale migration begins and ends in the warm waters of Mexico's Magdalena Bay. They have to avoid predators such as orcas, and obstacles such as oil tankers and pollution, as they travel 12,400 miles (20,000 km). This is the world's longest migration.

It's the middle of March. A juvenile male gray whale is ready to begin his first migration without his mother. Last year, he was a newborn whale and made the long journey at his mother's side. This year, he is old enough to travel with the other male gray whales. Gray whales travel together in groups called pods. The pods begin their migrations at different times.

The newly pregnant females were the first to begin their migration.

Tourists in Mexico can get very close to the whales.

Now, the older male grays are ready to leave. The juvenile will travel with the adult males and other young gray whales. Newborns and their mothers will stay in the warm Mexican waters for a few more weeks. The newborns need to feed so they can put on weight for their long journey north.

As they travel, the gray whales must keep an eye out for killer whales. Also known as orcas, these predators travel in pods and hunt migrating gray whales. Orcas prefer to attack younger gray whales, like our juvenile. Monterey Bay in California is known as "Ambush Alley" because so many orcas wait for the migrating grays and attack them as they swim across the bay's open water.

The juvenile avoids the pods of orcas and, by early May, he arrives off the coast of Oregon in the United States. He has swum more

Black-and-white orcas lie in wait to strike the whales.

than 1,000 miles (1,600 km) with his pod. For some grays, this is where the journey ends.

Each year, between 200 and 300 gray whales stay for the season in these coastal waters. There is enough food to support a few hundred gray whales, but our juvenile knows the real feast is farther north near Alaska. He continues on his migration.

Baleen
Gray whales feed on the ocean floor.
They suck in dirt, water, amphipods,
and krill. A substance in their
mouths called baleen acts like a
filter that catches the amphipods.

It is now June. The juvenile and
the other males in his pod arrive at
the Bering Sea off the coast of Alaska.
He has not eaten since beginning his
journey. He has been living off his fat
and now he is hungry!

The shallow waters off the coast
of Alaska are the feeding grounds for
thousands of gray whales. Gray whales
feed on amphipods and krill—tiny
marine animals that live on the ocean
floor. It takes about 660 pounds (300 kg)
of the tiny creatures to fill a gray
whale's stomach. During his stay here,

the juvenile eats about 73 tons (66 metric tons) of amphipods and krill and puts on a lot of weight.

Soon, it is October and the Arctic water is getting cooler. Before it freezes, the whales must journey south, back to the warmer waters

Krill is a big part of the gray whale's diet.

in Mexico, where the adults will breed.

Whales can get trapped in the ice if the Arctic freeze comes unusually early.

The whales can be seen off the
Canadian and U.S. coasts as they return
to Mexico's warm waters. The juvenile
will spend the winter near Mexico,
but he won't eat during these winter
months. Instead, he will live off the fat
reserves gained from feasting in summer.

Starting in December, thousands
of adult gray whales will mate in the
shallow lagoons along the coast of
California and Mexico. Thirteen months
later, during the next winter, females

will give birth to the calves conceived this December.

Pregnant females and a helper whale, called an "auntie," will swim to shallow nursery lagoons to give birth. The newborn gray whales will grow fast. In spring, like generations before them, these newborns will start their very first migration north to feed in Alaska.

Snow geese

A blustery breeze blows along the northeast coast of Baffin Island in Canada's Arctic. Thousands of white-feathered birds nest on the island's rocky shore. They are greater snow geese and they are getting ready to begin their fall migration. They fly 2,500 miles (4,000 km) south to escape the cold Arctic winter. During this migration, they fly in flocks as large as 1,000 birds. The following

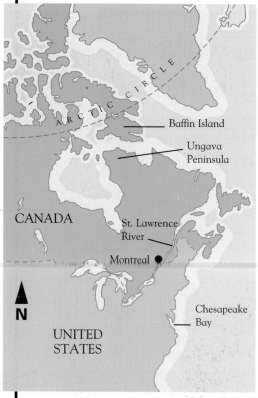

Snow geese migrate from Baffin Island to around Chesapeake Bay, and back.

ARCTIC CIRCLE

Baffin Island

Ungava Peninsula

CANADA

St. Lawrence River

Montreal

N

Chesapeake Bay

UNITED STATES

Snow geese migrate south in the fall.

spring, they will migrate north to the Arctic in flocks of a few hundred.

Greater snow geese are completely white, except for black feathers on their wingtips. Their bills have cutting edges that help them feed on plants growing on muddy river banks. They live only in the eastern part of North America.

It is the first week of September. The Arctic days are getting shorter, and the nights much colder. Soon, the ground and water on Baffin Island will freeze. For the snow geese, it is time to begin their migration. They will fly south to the eastern coast of the United States.

Two young snow geese, called goslings, test their wings on a strong

breeze. They were born in July. For two months, their parents have protected them from predators such as Arctic

The fur of Arctic foxes begins to turn white in the fall to help them blend in with the snow in winter.

foxes, gyrfalcons, and jaegers. Now, they must be strong enough to make the long journey south.

The goslings will fly close to their parents as they travel. The goslings' mother and father will watch over them as they fly south.

A strong breeze blows onto the shore. The goslings' parents take flight. The goslings are quick to join them in the air. The long fall migration has begun!

By the middle of September, the two little goslings, their parents, and the rest of the flock have flown more than 620 miles (1,000 km) across Baffin Island and have landed on the Ungava Peninsula in northern Quebec. For several days, they will feed and gain

their strength. Then they will continue their journey south for another 620 miles (1,000 km), over the Canadian forest, to the St. Lawrence River.

It is now the middle of October. The goslings and the rest of their flock stay by the St. Lawrence for 20 days, feeding to regain their strength.

When they are strong enough, the snow geese continue on their migration to their wintering grounds in the United States, more than 1,200 miles (2,000 km) away to the south. Will the goslings be able to keep up?

It is early November when the goslings and their parents arrive at Chesapeake Bay, on the eastern coast of the United States. They, and thousands of other snow geese, will spend the winter here.

In March, the goslings are bigger and ready to begin the spring migration north, back to their home on Baffin Island. On the way, they will stay for more than a month on the south shore of Lac Saint-Pierre, near Montreal, Canada.

The snow geese start to arrive back on Baffin Island in June. The goslings are not even a year old and they have already traveled nearly 5,000 miles (8,000 km). The adult snow geese will mate and raise their young during the summer, while our goslings will continue to grow. When the cold winds return to Baffin Island, they will be ready to lead the next generation of snow geese on the long migration south.

Effects of humans

One hundred years ago, there were only 3,000 greater snow geese left. Now, there are nearly a million. The numbers have increased partly because people passed strict hunting laws and created bird sanctuaries.

But humans are not always so helpful. Sometimes they add to the many dangers faced by migrating animals on their long journeys.

Oil companies want to drill for oil in the calving grounds of the Porcupine caribou herd. We all use oil, and drilling in Alaska provides jobs for local people. But it also changes the land forever.

Scientists predict that the Porcupine herd will stop migrating to the calving grounds if drilling is allowed, and they say there is nowhere else for the caribou to give birth safely.

The Arctic National Wildlife Refuge was created to protect the caribou and other animals in the region. Oil companies have asked for permission to drill there. Do you think they should be allowed to?

Long oil pipelines like these might affect the annual migrations of many animals.

The gray whale migration is made more dangerous because of humans.

Oil companies blast air into the sea floor in search of buried oil, and the military uses sonar to track submarines. Both these activities make a lot of noise underwater. Scientists think the noise can confuse gray whales, sending them into shallow water where they get stranded. And migrating gray whales

This stranded whale was returned back to the ocean.

can be injured or even killed if they collide with ships.

Humans also affect the monarch butterfly migration. Construction of roads, houses, and other buildings takes away trees that provide valuable roosting spots for migrating monarchs. And when people dig up milkweed plants from their gardens, or spray them with pesticides, they remove a vital food source for monarchs.

Fortunately, butterfly sanctuaries across North America provide safe havens for monarch butterflies. And you can help, too. Create a butterfly-friendly garden by planting milkweed in your backyard. You'll be feeding monarchs and you'll be taking part in an amazing animal migration.

Glossary

Antlers
Bony stalks that grow from some animals' heads.

Amphipods
Tiny creatures that live on the ocean floor.

Behavior
The way that an animals acts.

Caterpillar
The wormlike larva of a butterfly.

Chrysalis
The thin sac in which a caterpillar changes into a butterfly.

Directional flight
Flying in one direction as opposed to flying around to various different points.

Dormant
Among plants or animals, the state of being asleep for a long time.

Jaeger
A gull-like bird from northern Canada.

Juvenile
An animal that is older than a baby, but not yet an adult.

Krill
Tiny crustaceans that live on the sea floor and are eaten by whales.

Lagoon
A small body of water attached to a larger ocean or sea.

Larvae
Baby insects.

Lichen
A mix of fungus and algae that grows on rocks or flat ground and looks like a thin, colorful carpet.

Migration
A movement of animals that takes place year after year in the same season, to and from the same place.

Nutritious
Providing materials needed to help an animal grow.

Orca
A killer whale.

Pesticides
Chemicals sprayed on plants to kill unwanted insects.

Plain
A flat, wide, usually treeless area of land.

Pod
A group of whales.

Predator
An animal that hunts and kills other animals.

Rut
The mating season of antlered animals such as caribou, moose, and deer.

Sanctuary
An area of land in which animals are protected from human harm.

Sonar
A system that uses sound waves to detect movement under the water.

Tundra
Large, open areas of the Arctic where the soil is frozen and no trees grow.

Index